CREATESPACE

INTERIOR FILE FORMATTING GUIDE

Using

(How to Format Your Print-on-Demand Paperback Without Looking Dumb)

ABRAHAM ADEKUNLE

CreateSpace Interior File Formatting Guide Using Microsoft Word

(How to Format Your Print-on-Demand Paperback Without Looking Dumb)

Copyright © 2018 Abraham Adekunle

ISBN-13: 978-1720328278

ISBN-10: 1720328277

First edition: May 2018

10 9 8 7 6 5 4 3 2 1

*To Elizabeth Adams Tivel who found me out
and makes me feel worthwhile every time. This isn't
goodbye.*

CONTENTS

INTRODUCTION

For some time now, I've watched cash strapped authors lament how they waste their precious time learning the ropes of how to format—or design, if you will—their print-on-demand interior files.

Some use Open Office and swear by the 77 gods of technology that they'll never open that software again. A tiny percentage masters process after investing a couple of hours every day. But majority weren't. (Trust me, I know how multitudes run to software like Scrivener and Vellum. I'm not against using them, by the way.)

Some use Microsoft Word and ended up confused more than they were at the beginning. Again, another tiny percentage masters the process.

Others. Others who have cash to spare pay professionals to design their interior files or buy software they can use repeatedly.

But what about you? The writer who's just starting out. The one with a few book under his or her belt. The one who can't spare a couple hundred bucks yet for interior file formatting. Wouldn't you like to spend more of your time writing than worrying about how to use a program? Wouldn't you like to have a step-by-step guideline on how to format your interior file in the familiar Microsoft Word?

Hello, my name is Abraham Adekunle, and I just want to share the little knowledge I have on interior file formatting with you. I wrote my first book at 17 with little support. So, I had to roll up my sleeves and invest hours every day into learning how to do various things, one of which is how to format paperbacks in Word.

And the good thing is that you don't have to do that again. In this book, I *hold* your hand and show you step-by-step with illustrations how to do it. In fact, if you want to make it a routine where you just print the instructions, hang it on a wall, and follow them whenever you need them, you're covered. Also, I've tried to make the illustrations in this book as visual as possible. I'm a visual learner, I know.

I've tried to make this book as succinct as can be, because I know that you'd rather be writing than reading a 400-page book.

Notices

All the steps mentioned in this book are based on the 2007 version of Microsoft Word. The steps should be similar in your version of Word if you have a newer version.

I wrote this book with CreateSpace in mind, because I self-publish my paperbacks with the CreateSpace Independent Publishing Platform. But I believe formatting your interior file for any other print-on-demand platform such as Lulu or IngramSpark will still be the same.

In chapter six, I explained how I used the Nitro Reader 3 to export my PDF files. This isn't a sponsorship ad or affiliate marketing. I'm just a user.

ONE

PATTERN

What are the conventions you have to follow?

What do you notice first when you open a paperback book, be it fiction or non-fiction? The title, right? Most of the time, it's as big as the one on the front cover. Also, the title page includes the long subtitle which may not be on the front cover.

In summary, the title page contains:

- The book title in the same font and font size as on the front cover.
- The long detailed subtitled which may not be on the front cover.
- The author name(s) in the same font and sometimes the font size as on the front cover.
- The publisher or printing press. Many self-published books don't have this.

For the visual learners, here are examples:

CreateSpace Interior File Formatting Guide Using Word

What you've just seen is a pattern to be followed—not rules, because you can bend it. For instance:

- You may not include the subtitle.
- You may not include the press on the title page if you self-publish it.
- Some books, like the ones in the images above, have their title pages on the third page. The first page of a book begins on the right after opening the cover. Some first pages are left blank while others include only the book title in a small font at the middle of the page.

But one thing still remains true: there must be a title page at the beginning of every book. It's a pattern and no rule says it must be on the first or fifth page.

Have the following patterns in mind as you prepare to design your interior file:

a. The front matter and the back matter don't have headers and footers.

The front matter refers to the pages preceding the introduction, prologue, or first chapter of a book, as the case may be. The back matter refers to the pages following the conclusion, epilogue, or last chapter, as the case may be. This pattern has no exception.

Some authors or designers find a way to bend it by numbering the front and back matters in Roman numerals. You don't want to give yourself that headache except, of course, if you want to.

b. All chapters' first pages begin on the right.

This includes the introduction, epilogue, prologue, and conclusion. It means that the first pages begin on an odd number page.

c. Chapters' first pages have no header.

No title. No author name.

d. All chapters' pages are numbered.

The first page of a chapter has no header, right? But it must have a page number at the bottom of the page.

e. Blank pages are just that—blank!

No header or footer. Blank pages occur in the middle of a book because some chapters end on a page on the right. If you use a page break (Ctrl+Enter) or Next Page section break (Page Layout=>Breaks=>Next Page), the first page of the following chapter will fall on the right, an even page. A blank page is needed to shift the first page of that chapter to the right, an odd page.

You don't need to engineer a blank page. You just have to use an Odd Page section break (Page Layout=>Breaks=>Odd Page). If you follow this step, you'll never have to worry about how to handle blank pages again.

f. Book title headers are on the left pages while author name headers are on the right.

The left pages in MS Word are the even pages while the right pages are the odd.

For visual learners, I've prepared a PDF preview file where you can visualize the patterns. To download, check the Resources page at the end of this book. For you reading a paperback version, this book is a preview on its own.

TWO

STRUCTURE

Where does the formatting really happen?

Let's talk about the structure of an interior paperback in two ways:

- The trim size.
- The content.

The Trim Size

This includes the width, the height, and the margins of a book. The number of pages in a book determines the spine width, the thickness of the book.

These are common industry trim sizes:

- 5" width by 8" height.
- 5.5" width by 8.5" height.
- 5.25" width by 8" height.
- 6" width by 9" height.
- 8.5" width by 11" height.

CreateSpace Interior File Formatting Guide Using Word

Let's take a 5" by 8" trim size, for example. The following margins should be reasonable.

- 0.5" top and bottom margins.
- 0.5" or less outside margins.
- 0.5" or more inside margins.

Note: Because you're not formatting an everyday document, the type of margin you select should include the inside and outside margins. You're formatting two pages at a go. This is what it means:

: Top margin

: Bottom margin

: Inside margins (any dimension you choose here will be doubled to compensate for both pages)

: Outside margins (each on either side, as you can see)

In MS Word, go to Page Layout=>Size=>More Paper Sizes or Page Layout=>Margins=>Custom Margins.

In the Paper tab, insert your trim size in the width and height boxes. In the Margins tab, choose "Mirror margins" in the options for multiple pages. Then you can choose your top, bottom, outside, and inside margins.

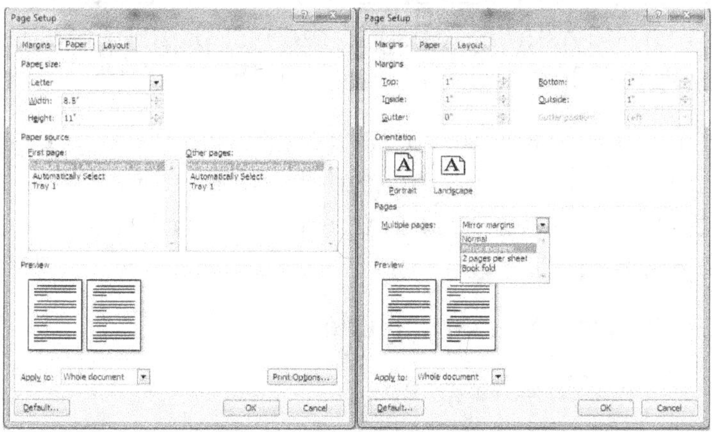

The Content

As I said earlier, there's a section popularly called the front matter. Another, the back matter. Now, we also have the actual content where the novel starts or the book begins.

The content of a book includes:

1. The front matter or section.
2. The actual content.
3. The back matter or section.

The Front Matter

This refers to the pages before the introduction, prologue, or first chapter. This is where CreateSpace, Lulu, or IngramSpark begins to count the number of pages of your book. But readers don't. They simply open to the last page of the last chapter and look at the page number.

CreateSpace, or any print-on-demand company, will not follow your custom-made page numbers because they will manufacture the whole book, not the numbered pages only.

The front matter includes:

- The title page.

- The copyright page.
- The dedication page.
- The acknowledgement page(s).
- The foreword page(s).

a. The title page.

As I said in chapter one, the title page includes the book title in the same font and font size, as on the front cover, the long detailed subtitle which may not be on the cover, the author name usually in the same font and font size, and sometimes the publisher or printing press.

Also, the title page shouldn't necessarily be on the first page of your book.

b. The copyright page.

This page comes immediately after the title page and is a page on the left. In other words, this page and the title page share the same leaf—title page on this side and the copyright page on the other.

The copyright page contains the book title, author name, year of publication, copyright notice, ISBN-10 and ISBN-13, and copyrighted works used in the book with permission. A much smaller font size is used.

CreateSpace Interior File Formatting Guide Using Word

Copyright pages are usually only a page. Brief and in smaller front sizes.

c. The dedication page.

This page also comes immediately after the copyright page and is a page on the right. It sometimes has no title to indicate as seen in the PDF preview file.

The text on the page could be italicized and place one-third down the height of the book. This page is optional. I mean, it doesn't determine your book sales. Again, you can decide to include it in the back matter.

d. The acknowledgement page(s).

This page is also optional and could be in the back section. This is where you mention those who have helped you in the process of writing the book. The frogs that hop to you with inspiration, the kite that gives you countless idea, the snakes that gave you that sparkling idea about how to use fear in your horror story.

Both fiction and non-fiction can have it.

e. The foreword page(s).

This is not the same as the introduction or prologue. It's an introduction written by another individual for the book. This should be in the front section. What's an introduction doing at the back of a book, anyway?

f. The table of contents.

This is a list of chapters and sections with their corresponding page numbers. All non-fiction books are expected to have one while it's better off not included in fiction.

The automatic table of content in Word would work as well as the manual hyperlink. To insert an automatic ToC, go to References=>Table of Contents and choose between the two options.

For this feature to work, you must use the heading styles in the Home tab.

CreateSpace Interior File Formatting Guide Using Word

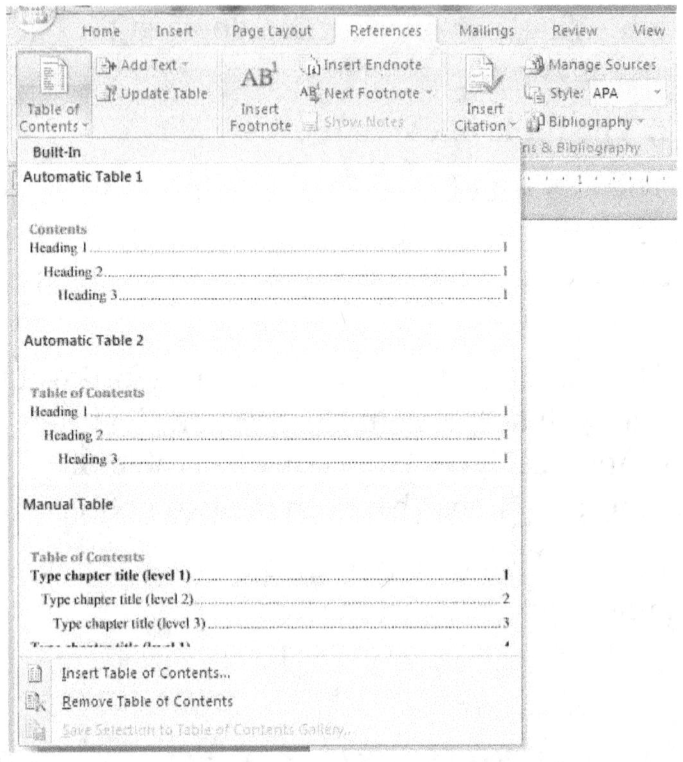

Now, do you remember pattern A in chapter one? The front matter refers to the pages mentioned above. They simply have no header or footer.

The Actual Content

This includes:

- Introduction or prologue.
- The chapters.
- Conclusion or epilogue.

Each of these three is numbered and has headers except the first pages.

The Back Matter

This refers to the pages following the last page of the epilogue, conclusion, or last chapter, as the case may be. CreateSpace, Lulu, and IngramSpark will also count the pages of this section. Many readers won't even check them.

The back matter includes:

- The acknowledgement page(s).
- The dedication page.
- Sales pitch page(s) e.g. other books by the author.
- Author's biography or note.

The first two items have been discussed in the front matter section, so, we'll move on to the third.

a. The sales pitch page(s).

This is where you introduce the other book(s) you've written. You can also promote your course(s) or program(s). This page(s) is/are optional.

b. The author's biography or note.

This is where you blow your horn. Write about yourself, your books, your achievements, your contacts, etc.

Do you still remember pattern A in chapter one? The back matter includes the above pages. They have no header or footer.

THREE

FOOTERS

How to format page numbers.

When I say "footer(s)," I'm referring to page numbers because that's what we'll be using it for. Footers can also be used for other purpose(s) if you so wish, but are mostly used for page numbers.

Having explained the content structure of a paperback interior, we'll need to apply the knowledge here.

Headers and Footers Work Like Cables

Every footer and header of every page is interconnected, but you can disconnect them in ways you like. Think of your entire book this way:

CreateSpace Interior File Formatting Guide Using Word

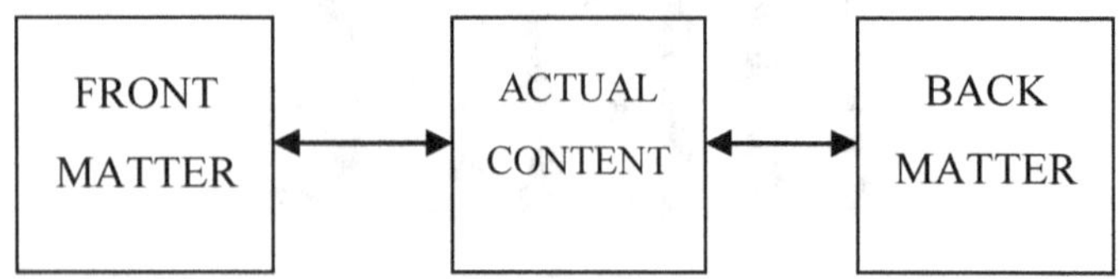

Before you can do anything at all, you need to disconnect the Actual Content from both the front and the back sections. After disconnection, you should view it this way:

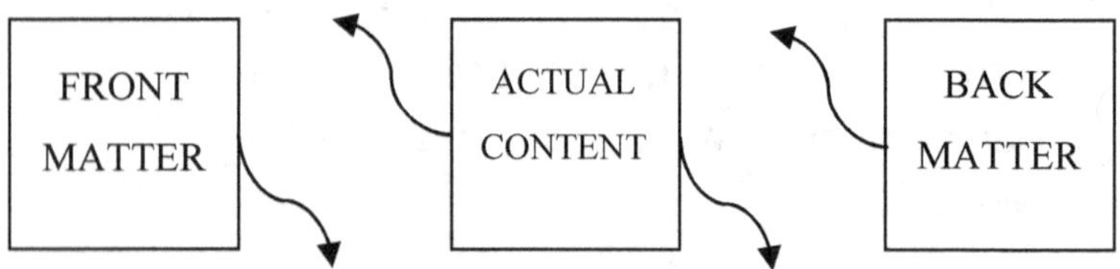

You can see in the above images that each has been disconnected from the others. But the question is how.

a. Replace all page breaks with section breaks.

Of course, I believe you know that you should use a page break when:

- You're crossing into another chapter.

- Other advanced purpose(s) (for advanced users.)

Typically, you might have:

- …used Ctrl+Enter to insert a page break;
- …used Insert=>Page break; or
- …pressed the Enter key repeatedly until you arrive at a new page.

None of those methods will work. In fact, the last one is worse as there's no distinction between the front and the back sections and the actual content. Even the actual content won't be distinguished by chapters. You need to go back and fix the errors.

To insert a section break, go to Page Layout=>Breaks=>Odd Page. Use this in place of the page breaks and you're now back on track.

Note: I recommend that you use an Odd Page section break because it handles blank pages. There are exceptions, though. For example, if you insert an Odd Page section break at the end of a title page, the next page (which is the copyright page) will shift to page 3 instead of being on page 2.

I'll advise you to use a Next Page section break (Page Layout=>Breaks=>Next Page) on the title page and continue to use Odd Page section breaks (Page Layout=>Breaks=>Odd Page) thereafter.

b. Disconnect the three sections.

After replacing the page breaks:

i. Move your cursor to the first page of introduction, epilogue, or first chapter.
ii. Double-click the footer area. A tab, Design, will come up.
iii. Tick "Different First Page" and "Different Odd & Even Pages."
iv. Deactivate "Link to Previous."

Now that first, odd, and even pages have been created, the linkage now looks thus:

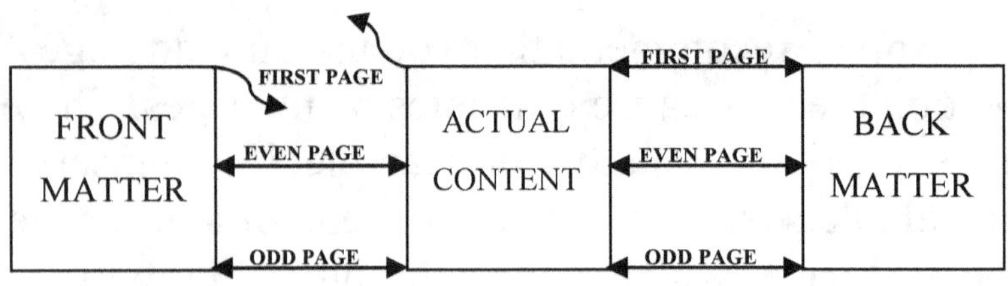

The First Page of the Actual Content has been disconnected from the front matter but not from the back matter (don't worry, we'll get to that.) That means any footer inserted on any First Page in the

Front Matter will not reflect on the Actual Content, but any footer inserted on any First page of the Actual Content will not only reflect throughout the Actual Content but on the Back matter.

So, let's disconnect the odd and even pages.

v.   Move your cursor to the footer of the next page (which will be even) and deactivate "Link to Previous."

vi.   Move your cursor to the footer of the next page (odd) and deactivate "Link to Previous."

Now, the Front Matter has been disconnected from the Actual Content. Let's do the same for the Back Matter, too.

vii.   Move your cursor to the first page of the Back Matter. (It could be Acknowledgement, Other Books, or Dedication. Whichever one comes first.)

viii.   Double-click on the footer area. Tick "Different First Page" and "Different Odd & Even Pages."

ix.   Deactivate "Link to Previous" on the footer of the First Page, Even Page, and Odd Page. If there's no Odd Page, search for the next Odd Page. It could be under

Author's biography. If there's none, then don't worry about that.

If you've followed these steps carefully, you've successfully unlinked the actual content from the front and the back sections.

Since we don't need headers or footers in those sections, let's simply face the actual content.

Formatting the Page Numbers

a. Create more First Pages.

You should remember that you ticked "Different First Page" when unlinking both the front section and the back section from the actual content. You need to create more throughout the actual content.

   i.   Move your cursor to the chapter after the introduction, prologue, or first chapter. Whichever one. For example, if your book starts with an introduction, you'll move your cursor to chapter one. If your book starts with chapter one, you'll move your cursor to chapter two.

   ii. Double-click on the footer area. In the Design tab, tick "Different First Page."

"Different Odd & Even Page" has been activated throughout the document.

iii. Do not deactivate "Link to Previous." If you do that, it means you're slicing the Actual Content section like bread.

iv. Repeat i-iii for the remaining chapters, epilogue or conclusion included.

b. Start numbering.

Now the Actual Content is now ready to be numbered. Here's how:

i. Go to the First Page of the first chapter (introduction, prologue, or chapter one. Whichever.)

ii. Double-click on the footer area.

iii. In the Design tab, go to Page Numbers=>Format Page Numbers. A window will pop up.

iv. In the section tagged "Page numbering," select "Start at" and input 1 in the box in front of it. Click on OK.

v. Go to Page Numbers and choose "Plain number 2." A page number will appear on every First Page of the Actual Content.

vi. Move your cursor to the footer of the even page. Go to Page Numbers and choose "Plain number 2."

vii.　　Move your cursor to the footer of the odd page. Then go to Page Numbers and choose "Plain number 2." Save your work.

The page numbers will be centered and will have traveled across the Actual Content section.

Congratulations! You have just formatted the page numbers of your book.

FOUR

HEADERS

How to format title and author name headers.

Headers refer to the book title and author name on top of the pages of your book. The book title goes on the left pages (even) while the author name goes on the right (odd) pages. The First Page of every chapter simply has no header.

Some books use chapter titles in the appropriate chapter instead of book title or author name.

Of course, the header also works like the footer. It's still the same as:

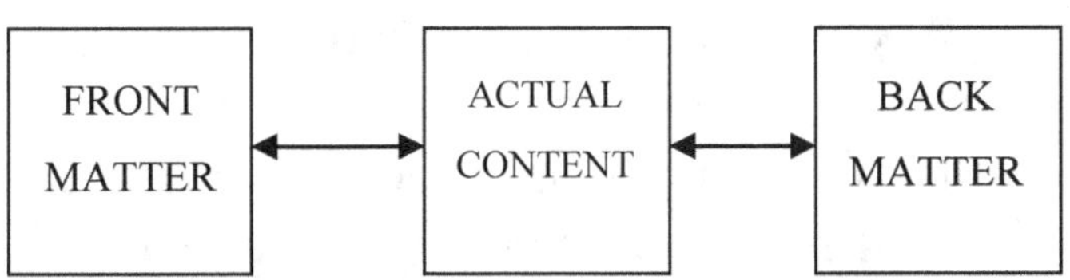

When unlinked, you can still visualize it as:

CreateSpace Interior File Formatting Guide Using Word

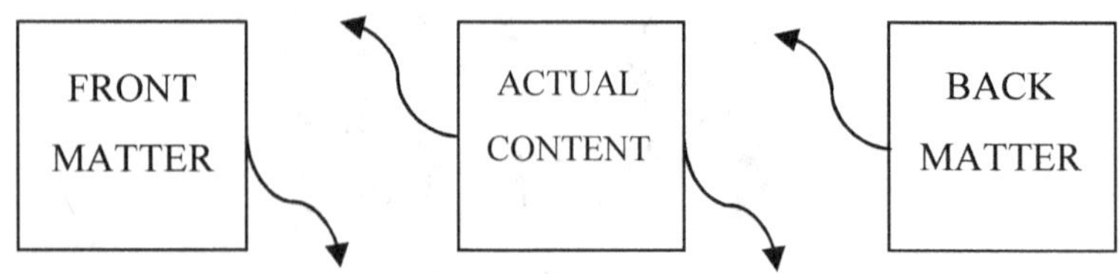

So, the steps for the disconnection are still the same. Since all page breaks have been replaced with section breaks, we move a step forward.

a. Unlink the Front Section.

    i.   Move your cursor to the first page of the first chapter, introduction, or prologue. Whichever, as the case may be.

    ii.   Double-click on the header area.

    iii.   Since First, Even, and Odd Pages have been created in the previous chapter, there's no need for that again.

    iv.   Deactivate "Link to Previous."

    v.   Move your cursor to the header of the next page (even page) and deactivate "Link to Previous."

    vi.   Move your cursor to the header of the next page (odd page) and deactivate "Link to Previous."

b. Unlink the Back Section.

   i.   Move your cursor to the first page of the back matter. This is the page immediately after the last page of the last chapter, conclusion, or epilogue, as the case may be.

  ii.   Double-click on the header area.

 iii.   Deactivate "Link to Previous."

 iv.   Do the same for the headers of the next two pages (even and odd pages.)

Formatting the Headers

a. The book title.

   i.   Move your cursor to any Even Page in the Actual Content.

  ii.   Double-click on the header area.

 iii.   Press Ctrl+E to centralize.

 iv.   Write your book title in all CAPS. Save your work.

b. The author name.

   i.   Move your cursor to any Odd Page in the Actual Content.

  ii.   Double-click on the header area.

 iii.   Press Ctrl+E to centralize.

 iv.   Write the author name as on the cover in all CAPS. Save your work.

CreateSpace Interior File Formatting Guide Using Word

Congratulations! You have successfully formatted the headers of your interior file.

FIVE

STYLES

How do you work with styles?

One of the fears of a DIY author about formatting a paperback interior file is that they might have to design certain headers repeatedly. The sudden realization that formatting isn't about headers and footers only. How do you style 35 chapter headings collectively, without having to do it one-by-one? Is it even possible?

Many authors, because they don't know how styles work, don't want to invest time they could channel to another productive task, or are afraid of getting their hands dirty, design the 35 chapter headings one-by-one. How long would that take? An hour? Two?

But the good news is that you can do it in ten minutes or less, depending on how fast you are. And the better news is that you don't have to invest your precious time running around in circles or get your hands dirty. I've done that and I'll carry you along every step of the way.

What is Style in Word?

How do you create new styles or modify existing ones? When do you use styles? When is style not necessary? Does it also have a learning process?

Those were the questions I kept asking myself when I realized that I had to learn to use styles. And every book I read on formatting paperback interior files, those were part of the questions I searched answers for.

Styles in Word is a set of design terms which you can apply to similar places in a document. Think of styles as a T-shirt. Same color, same design, same material, but different sizes. The size doesn't make the fashion designer alter the design. Only the size will be altered. That means a 5-year-old kid can wear a T-shirt of the same color, material, and design as a 35-year-old man. The only difference would be the size.

The same in Word. If you set the color of a particular paragraph to blue and underline it, it doesn't matter where you apply the style, it will set the color of that paragraph to blue and the text will be underlined.

In comparison, the design parameters stand for the same material, color, and design while the different texts stand for the sizes.

For instance, if you have a style named "Chapter Heading" and set the design as follow: bold centralized text, 20-point font size, Times New Roman font. And then you apply the style to the following chapter headings:

- Chapter one: beginning
- Chapter two: middle
- Chapter three: finishing

The text of those headings won't change, but the design will be the same. All the three headings will be in Times New Roman font, 20-point font size, emboldened and centralized text.

When is Style Necessary?

Using styles in Word isn't compulsory. In fact, if you decide to design your book page-by-page and line-by-line, you'll still derive the same result: a formatted interior file.

But in my opinion, using style is necessary when you have to apply the same design to more than one place (like chapter headings) and when you want to use the automatic table of content feature. I advise against using styles if you want to apply it to just one place.

Without much ado, here are places I recommend you use styles:

- **Chapter headings.** Every designer tries to make the headings of every book he or she designs unique. But I've noticed a few things.
    a) The chapter headings are usually placed at the middle of the page or farther down. There are exceptions, but there'll still be some space before the headings. This is achieved by increasing the space before the paragraph.
    b) Some fiction books use normal 12-point font size for chapter headings while more non-fiction books have headings in larger font sizes.
    c) Some non-fiction books use more than one line for chapter headings while fiction book seldom use more than one. This is because the aim of a fiction book is to transfer

the attention to the story while non-fiction readers are so eager to solve their problems that the design of the chapter headings matters little to them. Of course, there's no rule here and there are countless exceptions.

- **Chapter sub-headings.** This also works like a chapter heading but within a chapter. There are limits to the font size that can be applied to these sub-headings, depending on trim sizes. Otherwise, it'll make the page look awkward.
- **Body of text.** The style automatically applied to the body of text in a Word document is called "Normal."
- **Quotes.** If your book has more than one quote in the body of text, I recommend that you design a style for the quotes.

Also, here are places I recommend you don't use styles:

- **The title page.** I recommend you design this page without using styles because you wouldn't need that style you would've designed anywhere in the document again.

CreateSpace Interior File Formatting Guide Using Word

- **The copyright page.** It's only a page and the only modification you'd need is the font size and maybe the font. Why bother with styles?
- **The dedication page.** This is usually not more than a paragraph of three or four lines. It'll take less than a minute to design.
- **Modifications you have to do manually.** For instance, after I'd designed the chapter headings of one of my books, I wanted to increase the font size of part of the text. I had to do it manually because you can't program a style with two font sizes in the same paragraph.

Other instances are drop CAPS, a few words in a beginning paragraph all CAPS, no indent for beginning paragraphs of another scene, etc. You can create a style for no-indent paragraphs, but only if they're many i.e. more than two.

How Do You Create New Styles or Modify Existing Ones?

First, Microsoft has predesigned default styles that come with every version of Word. Some of them are:

- **Heading 1:** This is usually used for chapter headings.
- **Heading 2:** This is usually used for sub-headings.
- **Heading 3:** This is usually used for headings under chapter sub-headings.
- **Heading 4:** This is the last in the hierarchy of headings and is usually used under chapter sub-sub-headings.

Only these four styles and new styles created based on them will reflect in the automatic table of contents.

- **Normal:** This is the style automatically applied to the body of text in a Word document.
- **Quote:** This is used for quote.
- **Title:** This style is predesigned to style book title pages but optional in my opinion.

a. How to modify existing styles.

    i.   Click on Home. In the tab, go to the Styles section.

    ii.   Click on the double downward arrow. It will show all the styles in the document.

    iii.   Right-click on the style you want to modify. Then click on Modify. The Modify Style window will pop up.

b. How to create new styles.

    i.   In the Home tab, go to the Styles section. Click on the double downward arrow to reveal all the styles.

    ii.   Click on the style you want to model to apply it to the current paragraph. (Without applying it first, you can't create a new style based on it.)

    iii.   Click on the double downward arrow again.

    iv.   Click on "Save Selection as a New Quick Style…" A window will pop up.

    v.   Name the new style whatever you like.

    vi.   Click on Modify. Another window will pop up where you can select your designs and save your new style. If you don't click on OK, your new style won't be saved.

c. Modifying your styles.

i. For chapter headings. Let's say you want to leave a lot of space before the heading, set it to Cambria, 25-point font size, centralized, bold, and color black, and leave a little space before the body of the text.

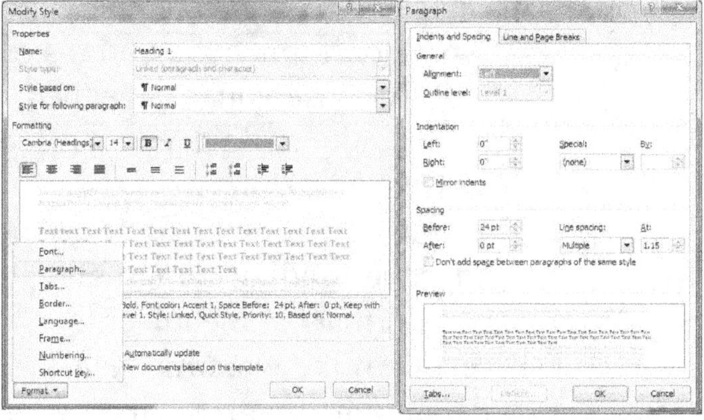

1) In the Modify window, choose the font, font size, alignment, bold or italics or underline formatting, and the color in the formatting section.
2) If you want a font size that's unavailable among the options, click inside the box and type in the desired size you want.
3) You can choose to embolden, italicize, and underline the same heading.

4) You can select whatever color you want because this isn't an eBook where you'll need Automatic color to adapt to the nature of the e-reader.
5) Choose the alignment below the font. Don't touch the options on its right because you'll have the opportunity to do that in a more flexible situation.
6) To modify the space before or after the heading paragraph, click on "Format" at the lower left corner of the window, then Paragraph. Another window will pop up where you can edit every paragraph formatting for that style.
7) In the Spacing section, increase the unit in the "Before" box to 100 points and above, depending on the amount of space you want. It could be 60 points as well as 150 points.
8) Set the unit in the "After" box to at least 6 points for readability. Also tick the "Don't add space between paragraphs of the same styles"

box. You don't want to have a 100-point space between your headings if they're more than a paragraph.

9) Set the line spacing to "Single" but you can also set it to whatever you want. If you choose "Single," leave the "At" box empty.

10) Set the "Special" box under Indentation to "none" and leave the "By" box empty. This is because it's a header and centralized.

11) When you're done, click OK. The window for modifying paragraph styles will disappear. Click on OK in the remaining window. Save your work. The changes you've made would have appeared throughout the book where that heading style has been applied.

ii. For chapter sub-headings, modify the styles as explained above. You can control the indent, line spacing, paragraph spacing, font, font size, alignment, etc. The good thing is that there's a preview screen where you'll see how the changes will look when it goes live.

iii. Images can only be formatted one-by-one. Insert an image by going to Insert=>Picture and selecting the image.

1) After the image has been inserted, click on Compress Pictures in the Format tab. A window will pop up.

2) Click on Options and tick "Automatically perform basic compression on save." Leave the "Target out" at "Print (220 ppi)." Click OK.

3) Click OK again and save your work.

4) To apply designs to the image, all you need are in the Format tab.

5) To apply border to the image, click on "Picture Border" and select the color of the border you want. Click on Picture Border again, then "Weight" to increase or decrease the size of the border.

6) To change the position of the image, click on "Text Wrapping" and choose from the options.

I. **In Line with Text:** is default for newly-inserted images and means Word will treat the image like text.

II. **Square:** is used when you want text to wrap around the image but want to be able to choose the margins (distance from text) all round.

III. **Tight:** This is similar to "Square" but you can only choose the distance from text on the left and on the right. The top and bottom margins will be determined by the styles applied to the preceding and the following paragraphs.

IV. **Through:** means that if there are transparent spaces in the image, text will pass through it.

V. **Top and Bottom:** No text wraps around the image. You can only choose the distance from text at the top and bottom of the image.

VI. **Behind text:** means the image will be sent to background.

Commonly used when designing a cover in Word.

VII. **In front of text:** means the image will cover the text like placing a picture on a book.

7) To apply a shape to the image, click on "Picture Shape" and choose. Some part of the image may be cropped out to achieve the chosen shape.

8) To apply effects to the image, click on "Picture Effects" and choose any one of "Preset," "Shadow," "Reflection," "Glow," "Soft Edges," "Bevel," and "3-D Rotation."

9) To rotate the image or flip it, click on Rotate.

10) To crop some part of the image, click on Crop.

11) You can also use the "Brightness," "Contrast," "Recolor," "Compress Pictures," and "Reset Picture" in the Adjust section. The "Change Picture" option is for replacing the currently selected image.

Note: If you need to apply the same custom style to more than two places in your interior file, you should probably create a new style or modify an existing style for it.

If you've also modified any style after formatting your headers and footers, I assure you that nothing will change except you delete a section break. If more pages are created, the page numbers and the headers will fall in place.

SIX

PDF

Exporting your file into PDF.

Exporting your interior file into PDF isn't as easy as using the Save As option and converting the Word file using the SaveAsPDF addon.

For instance, CreateSpace expects and requires you to embed necessary fonts in your PDF file, which the SaveAsPDF addon cannot do. Also, images you insert in your file should be at least 300 dpi or ppi.

I've tried using a version of Adobe Reader for this, but it functioned only as a PDF reader, not as a PDF printer. That means you can't request that the program print a document to PDF.

The PDF reader I use that also functions as a PDF printer is Nitro Reader 3 (please, search for the software on Google.) It views PDF files and also creates from Word, Excel, PowerPoint, and even the internet.

CreateSpace Interior File Formatting Guide Using Word

So, I'll teach you how to export to PDF with Nitro Reader 3. (If you use any other program or a newer version of Word that can export to PDF, you can use it if the files it produces meet CreateSpace's requirements.)

From here on, I'll assume that you have installed Nitro Reader 3.

    a. In Word, go to Print=>Print or simply press Ctrl+P. The Print window will pop up.

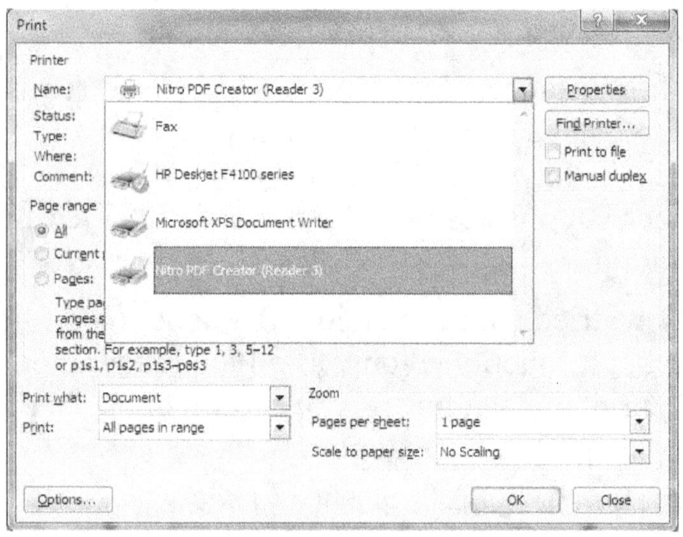

    b. Choose Nitro Reader 3 as your printer. Then click on properties. Another window will pop up.

c. In the first tab, choose the Target folder (where you want to save the file) and the version of the PDF file you want to create.

d. In the "Conversion Quality" section, select "Custom." The "Options" button will become available. Click on it.

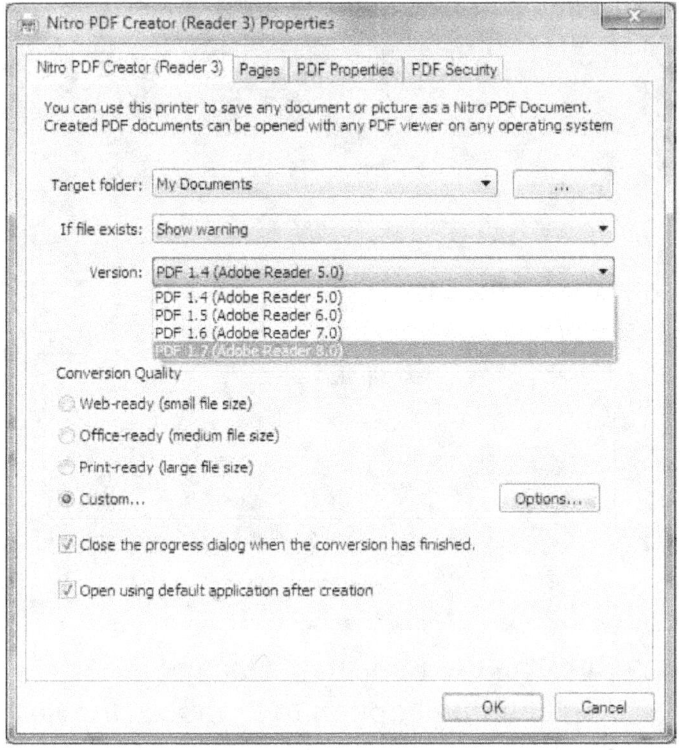

e. Another window will pop up. In the Images tab, if you want to convert all the color images you've inserted in the file to grayscale, tick "Convert color images to grayscale." Otherwise, Downsample it to at least 300 dpi and change the Image quality to High.

f. If you want to convert grayscale images to monochrome or downsample monochrome images, apply step (e).

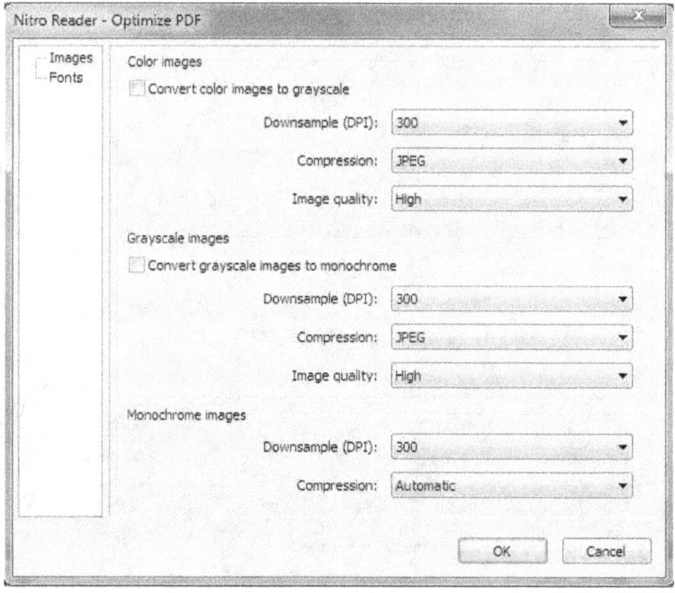

g. Click on the Fonts tab. Change the "Embedding" option to "Embed (Fullset)" and "If embedding fails" choose "Cancel job." You can decide to embed base 14 fonts or not, but I like to embed them to avoid having to go re-embed them if CreateSpace requires it. Click on OK.

h. Click on the Pages tab, then Custom Forms. A window containing the list of saved custom-page sizes will pop up. If your book's trim size isn't on the list, click on Add.

i. Name the form and input your book's width and height in the appropriate boxes. Click on OK.

j. Select the newly-created page size and click OK.

k. If you wish to include a metadata, click on the PDF Properties tab. Don't include any form of security because the file may be rejected.

l. Click on OK when you're done. Then click on OK in the Print window to create your print-ready PDF file.

CreateSpace Interior File Formatting Guide Using Word

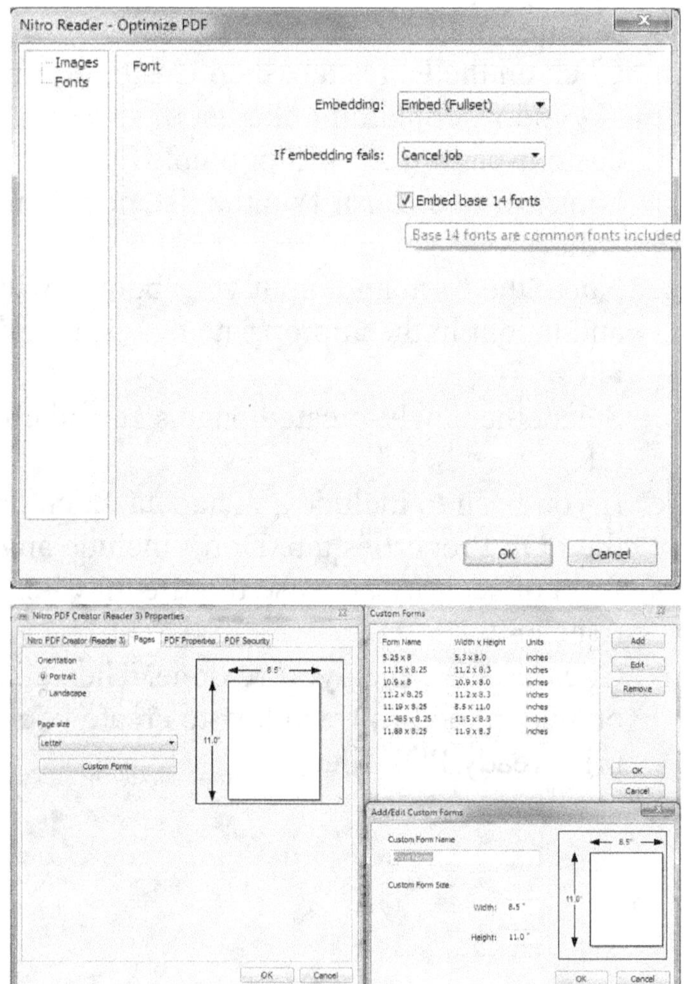

FEEDBACK

I've made this book as short as it could be, but I'm willing to add more content to it if you're willing to ask questions based on your level of understanding.

My goal is to add a Question-and-Answer chapter where important issues can be resolved,

Please, forward all correspondence to Abraham@abrahamadekunle.com

If you have no question or suggestion, a review of the book will be much appreciated.

RESOURCES

MS Word 2007: The guidelines in this book are based on the 2007 version of Microsoft Word. The steps are similar for newer versions.

Nitro [PDF] Reader 3: This doubles also as my Word-to-PDF converter. It embeds necessary fonts to meet CreateSpace's interior PDF file requirements. The installation file only supports Windows 7 64-bit OS. Please, find other versions compatible with your OS.

PDF Preview File: This is the PDF I created for visual learners to help them understand how a paperback interior file should be formatted. It also contains the listed patterns in chapter one of this book.

Interior File Sample: This is the Word of the truncated version of this book's interior file. I've made it in .doc and .docx formats to avoid compatibility issues.

To download **Nitro Reader 3, the PDF Preview File, and the Interior File Sample,** go to: https://bit.ly/2KVmj5S

OTHER BOOKS

What if you could learn how to write a story from scratch? What if you could build in-depth characters, settings, and conflicts that catch readers' mind and build suspense? What if you could avoid writing jargon altogether, even while writing exclusively for yourself? Learn *How to Write a Short Story* now.

Should you jump in front of the keyboard and start writing? Or take your time to outline? How do you balance writing and publishing faster with taking time to plan and outline? Learn how in *Plan, Research, and Outline Your*

Acknowledgement

Thank you, Bridgette Anne Stine for giving me the needed push to write this book and for your invaluable feedbacks.

About The Author

Abraham Adekunle is a young writer from a Lagos suburb in Nigeria.

He is the author of *How to Write a Short Story; Plan, Research, and Outline Your Nonfiction Book in a Day; A Hunt: A Military Crime Thriller;* and *The Chase: A Military Crime Thriller.* They are available as eBooks and paperbacks on Amazon.com

Being tech savvy, Abraham knew that if he was to publish his books as both eBooks and paperbacks, he would have to roll up his sleeves and get to serious work.

Now, although still young and with little support, he has invested time and mastered DIY self-publishing tasks such as cover design, print-on-demand interior file design, print-on-demand full print PDF cover, etc.

He is on a mission to share his knowledge with writers, especially non-natives.